Collected Poems, Vol. I

# *A Beautiful Suffering*

John Mulhall

Printed in the United States of America

1st Printing, 2018

Published by Blanket Fort Books

Softcover ISBN: 978-1-7324374-1-8
eBook ISBN: 978-1-7324374-0-1

johnmulhall.com
facebook.com/authorjohnmulhall

Cover design and layout by Grant England
Cover and author photography by Victor Lightworship
Body painting by Luciano Paesani
Cover models are Clarissa Swallows and Cesar Castillo
Curation by Holly McKinley
Editing by Cheryl Armstrong

For my good friend
Wendy Cherry,
for your love, support,
and inspiration.

# A Word from the Writer

I am a storyteller.

That's how I answer when people ask me when I knew I wanted to be a writer. I didn't really ever make a decision to put pen to paper for purposes of a career. I just knew I liked telling stories, that people around me seemed to think I was pretty good at telling stories, and more, that I had stories to tell. So, whether that meant I was going to be a writer or a filmmaker or a songwriter or some other type of creative, I just knew that I wanted to be a storyteller.

On that subject, I've never presumed to consider myself a "poet," per se. The esteemed poets I know and respect are all thoroughly educated professionals, with a deep understanding of the mechanics, the nuance, and the history of the art form. And I am...not that. I have only been remedially educated about poetry and I have a rather shallow and workmanlike understanding of form and history.

What I do know is that I love words. I love the music of language. I love that when I desire to express some concise thing, some isolated thought or feeling or moment, I know that I have this toolbox full of vocabulary to use, and that I can string words together in such a way as to express myself in a somewhat melodic fashion. And that people who read them seem to respond to them.

But, regardless, I still consider myself a storyteller, using the magic of short-form – in this case, poetry – to tell my stories. And so, I offer my respect to the true professional and educated poets out there. I am a mere intruder playing in your esteemed sandbox. Believe me, I recognize my limitations. And you have my esteem.

I'd like to offer a few words of thanks to the people in my life who helped shape this collection. To those who offered feedback – Wendy Cherry, Megan Taylor, Lindy Larsen, Michelle Rowlett, Dayna Davis, Wendy Morales, and others – thank you! Holly McKinley, thanks for helping me winnow a large pile of poems into something more manageable and for all your help with curating this collection. To this day, I think you're likely the only person who has read all (or most) of my poems, and you have my apologies for some of them.

On the subject of stories, I have discovered the hard way that, whereas people seem to understand that authors of long-form fiction are telling fabricated stories about fabricated people, there is an assumption that stories told in poem form are inherently autobiographical. As an example, one of my poems, *He Dies at the End,* is about a man suffering from a deep and desperate hidden depression. It was inspired by the death of comedian Robin Williams and posted to both my author account and personal account on Facebook. The number of people who reached out to me to make sure that I was okay was both heartwarming and a lesson to me that people often assume poetry is truth.

Well, I hope that there is truth in all of my writing. But sometimes, that may just be a broad universal truth, not my own historical truth. While some of these poems are as autobiographical as they come – my life, my loves, my lies, my limerences, my exquisite joys, and my beautiful suffering – just as many, if not more, are not. So, please enjoy them, react to them, relate to them if you are able. As Yeats said, "Let us go forth, the tellers of tales, and seize whatever prey the heart long for, and have no fear. Everything exists, *everything is true,* and the earth is only a little dust under our feet."

While a book of poetry is a definite tangent from my normal style and subject matter, I hope you enjoy the storytelling, nevertheless.

Until next time, friends, the journey matters.

*- John Mulhall, January 15, 2018*

# Contents

# Contents

# Waking the Dead

Sometimes
I wake in a haze,
and swear that I hear you singing
down the hall.

There was a moment...
I felt I saw your crooked smile
reflected in the shards of glass
that once held the lavender candle
by my bed.

A woman at the airport,
dressed in black, wearing sandals;
a shift of her hip, a flip of her hair
and she was you.

I smell you sitting next to me
in the darkness.

I hear your laughter
in crowded rooms.

I chase your memory
through shadows.

I continue to wait,
as I sit in the middle of the cluttered floor;
I continue to anticipate
the feel of your coarse fingertips
on my shoulder,
through my hair.

"Let it go, love...
let it go, and come to bed."

# Astronaut

The stars look so
different
without the noise
from other lights.

Standing
in the middle
of this dusty, red wasteland,
it feels like the sky,
the entire cosmos
is revolving around me,
taunting me.
And the vividness
only compounds
my isolation.

There is a desert
wilderness
as far as I can see
in every direction
and for a moment
it's hard
to remember
how I arrived here.

For a moment.

I kick a rock
but there is no noise,
no other hint of life.
Only the sound
of my own breathing
inside the suit.

I am
alone,
like I wanted to be,
an astronaut
on my own mission,
a pioneer
into the bleak, cold expanses
of a barren
and lifeless
and loveless
rock.

# Acquiesce

"What would it take?" you ask, curiously.

What would it take
to make me
acquiesce?

Well, I'm capricious
as you know...
and so
it would depend
on a great,
great
many
things...

the poutiness
        of your lips,
the lighting
        of the room,
the angle
        of your lithe body,
        draped across
        the sitting room chair,
the way your camisole
        hangs off
        your smooth shoulder,
the tension
        beneath your skin,
the shallowness
        of your breath,
the twist
        of a foot
        wrapped
        in high-heeled
        obstinance,
the smell
        of you,
the truth
        behind your eyes...

and my whim.

# Just a Taste

"Just a taste," I whisper.
As if I could handle any more.
As if I wouldn't be gripped,
be seized,
and find myself
lost
in your scent,
and your kiss,
and your gaze,
and your touch.

Just a taste.
Of you.
Of it.
Of this.
While I can still flee,
while I can still
escape the pull of you,
before I find myself
plunging
beneath the surface
of your warm lake,
drinking from the reservoir
of your flowing fountain,
plumbing the depths of you,
adrift in you,
awake
and aware
and addicted
to your
drug.

Just a taste,
I reason,
I bargain,
I lie.
Knowing full well
that one taste
of you
will not be enough,
will never be enough,
to satisfy,
to mollify,
to leave me full up,

replete and
quenched.

Just a taste
will never do,
I know.
I know.
For my thirst is strong,
and there is enough of you
to drink from,
enough of you to appease,
enough of you to sink into,
over and over,
more and more and more,
but never
ever
enough
to keep me from craving you
all over
again.

# Clock

I watch the clock tick by
        interminably
towards a time I know
you will not call.

I let myself anticipate you
        anyway.

I let myself feel the twist
in my stomach,
the hope in my heart,
        the gnaw.

Always hope with you,
where none is truly warranted.
But always hope.

I want to hold on to the wind,
I want to trap the air.

# Keep Dancing, Sweetheart

Keep dancing, sweetheart.
Keep your eyes closed,
feel the hands on your face.
The beat is hard now,
the music loud.
A tall glass of red…
to wash you clean
from a moment in time
when you were better than this…

but, don't ever think about me

Kiss them, baby,
let your eyes roll back.
Sweat on your lips,
blood through your veins.
Press them against you,
hard and tight,
until they crush the memories
of a life that you glanced
and a person you were…

but, don't ever think about me

Keep rolling, love.
Let your heart pump hard.
Out of focus,
but uncompromising,
no sacrifices.
Life moving fast enough
to outrun
your own memory.
And perhaps someday,
it will grow dim on its own,
like a dying ember on a wooden floor.
Tears in your eyes
as the lights flash, bass pounds.
And even when the music fades away,
it's only for a short time.

Keep dancing, sweetheart,
and don't ever think about me.

# Broken Machinery

Your words
rattle around in my memory
like loose parts in so much broken machinery,
scraping at the edges of my mind.

"This feels different," you said,
smiling at me just so,
welcoming me into the safety
of your perfect green eyes.

And I agreed.

Yet here we are,
only hours later,
and the sameness of past interactions,
the staleness of familiar motions,
the sadness of frayed edges
have set upon us like carrion feeders,
great looming birds
ready to pluck at the flesh
of our openness,
to tear the eyes from the sockets
of our vulnerability.

"This feels different," you had said.

And it did.

# Casual

"Casual, I suppose,"
I reply,
in response to your query.

It's a quick answer,
an easy one,
one you can digest,
one you can accept,
mostly,
though you may not want to,
though you may not like it,
though you may not appreciate
the implication of the word as it passes through the filters
you come readily
and happily
preinstalled with.

It's not the truth, though.
It's just easy.
A way to move on
from the subject matter,
to pacify
your curiosity
about me,
even though you may frown at the notion,
lament the designation,
walk away feeling superior and self-satisfied
about your new understanding of me,
and of my life,
so cleverly summed up,
so expertly crystallized
in one word.

But, it's not the truth, no.
Not my truth.
There is so much more to it,
so much more than this answer
might lead you to believe,
so many deeper feelings
I could express
if only I had the time
or the inclination
or the energy.
So much nuance
in how I choose

to see the world.
So many gray areas.
So much capacity
for affection,
for love.

And I feel bad,
somewhat –
not really,
not deeply,
but somewhat –
for buying in,
perhaps out of fatigue
of an old conversation,
for surrendering
to your predisposition,
for checking off a box
on your handy preprinted list
of acceptable answers,
when there are no boxes,
when the entire point is no boxes,
and when there will never be room for boxes
here.

# Satin Doll

Abandoned at the side
of a dirty green dumpster,
next to piles of refuse,
yesterday's news,
and other forgotten hand-me-down toys,
lies my satin doll.
Clear blue eyes, slowly coming undone.
Soft smooth skin, now marred,
riddled with subtle cracks and lines.

Hard to believe that someone
loved you once...
desperately,
passionately,
more than any other,
more than breathing.

Hard to believe that someone
held you tight,
and drifted off to sleep
with you in their arms,
feeling protected by your closeness.

What happened to you in between?
What path did your journey take?
And was it worth it in the end?

You've lain next to so many others since then.
Their stink perfumes you now,
their grime shades your features,
betraying the inherent beauty
of your form.

You were a prize,
and then you were a pincushion.
Now you lie next to empty soup cans,
as vermin scurry beneath you,
and scavengers pull the painted eyes
from your once perfect face,
my satin doll.

# Trail of Blood

I pull my coat tight,
and bite down hard against the
bracing pain,
and force a smile.
Just act normal, I whisper
to myself.
Just act normal,
and no one will know.

I laugh and
chat in a lively manner
and eat and drink,
wondering, all the while,
if the alcohol will make things worse,
but not enough to stop.
And I even dance
and kiss
and love,
once or twice,
and it all seems just fine,
and no one notices
at all
when I almost stumble,
when I almost collapse.

And I wince from time to time,
and I feel the sweat on my brow,
I wonder if I'm feverish,
and I feel the dampness permeate my shirt,
my nice shirt,
my new one,
blood from a wound
that won't seem to heal.

And as the night goes on,
I grow more and more
confident in my
confidence act,
more certain that I will go
unnoticed,
under the radar,
hiding in plain sight,
even as I grow more
and more fatigued
and pale

and sickly
and weak.

Until
at last
she takes my arm,
unflinching,
unafraid,
and leads me out of the room
and to the car
and away from the subterfuge,
away from lies,
to safer grounds
where I can be still
and where long suffering
wounds
can finally be
attended.

And all it took was her,
to look beyond my smile,
to listen behind my lies,
and to notice
the trail of blood
I'd been leaving
in my path
since I'd arrived.

# As You Go

You press
your lips
to mine
gently
and step
into
the light
of day,
hair tousled,
dress askew.

You smile
as you go,
and me,
I smile back,

but only on the outside.

# Honeysuckle

I like honeysuckle
and the way your eyes shine in candlelight

I like the moment the lights dim in a theatre
and the pout of your lips

I like the way time freezes as the rollercoaster descends
and the way your fingers brush my face

I've tasted love

Tasted it from your lips
Heard it as it floated in on gentle breath
as you whispered it in my ear
Felt it grow inside
like a pain, a fever
twisting in my gut
Undeniable

I've tasted love

briefly

like a dream…

I like honeysuckle
I like minor chords
I like strawberry sunsets

I miss you

# Mouths

There are those
mouths...
mouths that when
we kiss them,
press against ours
like a dead weight
and make us strain.
Mouths that cover
our lips
with heaviness,
that stifle
our breath,
and smother us
with desperate tongue,
and that manage,
somehow,
to be ponderous,
lifeless,
even claustrophobic,
in the midst
of an ostensibly
passionate act.

And then there are
the other kind.
The ones
that feel
like home.
The ones that are
like an umbilical cord,
like a extension
of our own bodies,
a part of us.
The mouths whose
kisses
feed us,
nurture us,
comfort us,
give us life,
fill us up
with renewed breath,
and connect so deeply,
they remind us
why we ever kissed
in the first place.

Mouths like yours.

# Willingly

Candles cast fitful shadows
on indistinct walls
as I come to you.

Stripped of pretense,
open and fragile,
I lay my burdens at your feet.
I do it willingly.

I hold you closer than I think I could,
still in our silence,
hopeful.

I kneel for you,
I defer.
I strip my power, my control
and lay it aside.
I do it willingly.

I trust where no trust is promised
because I want to,
because I need to.

I'm a witness
to you
and a grace,
that you hide behind fear.

I give you my strength,
and you take nothing from me...
because I choose to give.

Come to me now
and be still in this silence,
and be hopeful,
because it's alright
to be hopeful
from time to time.

# Surely

A man sits
and watches
the clock
tick
away
steadily,
ceaselessly.

He is
waiting for his
love
to return,
waiting for things
to be
how they were
once before,
when they were both
so happy,
when things
were perfect,
and life
made sense.

He sits
quietly
at the kitchen table,
waiting
for the phone
to ring,
recalling
her touch,
her laughter,
her smile,
desperately longing
for her
to remember
at last
all of those things
she most
surely
had forgotten.

A single dressing gown,
hung haphazardly
on the knob

of a hallway door,
still smells
like her
every time
he passes.

He catches a glimpse
of a face
in a dusty
bathroom
mirror,
and for a moment
doesn't recognize
his reflection
at all.
His eyes
are sunken,
his face
gaunt.
He couldn't
recall
so little hair,
so much gray
in his beard.

Surely
she will call
today,
soon,
finally.
And then
they would get back
to building a life
together
again.

Surely
she won't let this
remarkable
love
slip
away
for good.

Surely
today is the day
she will call.

# Unloaded

It's locked.

But, don't let the door stop you...
if you want to get in,
then find a way.

I'm just sitting here
in the dark
listening to the record skip
at the end of a song I've replayed
too many times
to count.

Really, don't let the door stop you...
your words won't reach me
from outside;
that porch has no presence,
the sound has no life,
it doesn't carry.

And words alone
mean nothing
to me
at this point
anyway.

I'm just sitting here,
quite harmless...
Oh, sure, there's a pistol in my lap...
but it's unloaded...
just for show,
I swear.

Just like you.

I'm sitting here,
and I think I'm really
beginning to be okay
with the numb;
it's getting familiar to me,
like an old friend.

Don't let the door stop you...
it wouldn't if you meant
anything you've ever said

to me;
you'd be through it like gauze,
you'd be ravenous to get to me.

But in the meantime,
I'm just sitting here
thinking about
the delicate balances,
and the missed moments,
and the decisions pondered over,
and argued,
and weighed,
until they lose
       all
         meaning.

No, the door won't stop you, precious.
It's just a door.
It's fragile,
and temporary;
it's an illusion more than a barrier.
You can huff
and puff
and blow it right down.

But by the time
you decide
I'm worth the effort,
       I just may
       have snuck out
       the back.

# Built For It

You are
built for this.

For sweat
and fire
and hunger.

You are
a finely tuned instrument,
polished and honed
and adroitly constructed.

Your back is taut,
fibrous,
strong,
ready and able
to support the weight
of me.

Your fingers are agile,
adept at interweaving themselves
with mine,
snaking through my hair,
around
the back of my head,
and finding
the most hidden of my
buttons and switches
and gears.

Your legs are long,
slender,
muscular,
agile and malleable,
built perfectly
to wrap
around my waist
just so,
to rest
neatly
beside your ears;
your toes point to heaven
as if
it's our final
destination.

Your eyes,
they are beacons,
pulling me in,
lighting my way,
holding me rapt,
steadfast.
They are perfect
liars,
promising perfect
things
to an imperfect
man
in an imperfect
place.

And your mouth,
filled with sweet venom,
it seals my fate with
each and every
delicious
kiss.

You are truly
a machine.
A perfect engine.
You are engineered.
A marvel.
Intricately formed.
Perfectly assembled.
A masterpiece.
And it is as if
you were built
for this very
fucking
thing.

# Infatuated

I wake up with her name
on my tongue
again,
wrapped
and hidden
inside each exhalation
like a secret.

Her face is there,
in my imagination
perfectly etched.
Her eyes,
sparkling,
a heady mix of innocence
and mischievousness;
her lips,
framing an imperfect
and intoxicating
smile;
the way her
soft hair,
all subtle curls,
dusted by the sun,
falls against
her clavicle;
these
are the first thoughts
my waking consciousness
will allow.

I think of her too much now.
She's like a riddle to me.
And as with any
good riddle,
any complex puzzle,
any compelling mystery,
I spend
countless
minutes
of each day
devoted
to figuring her out,
to figuring me out,
this near
infatuation

of her,
to turning the puzzle
of her
over
and over
in my mind.

I know
well enough
that no answer
truly awaits me.
But I allow myself
to relish
the thrill of exploration,
to crave
the moments when
she occupies
my thoughts,
and to long to awake
again
and again
with
her perfect
name
on my tongue.

# Candy from Strangers

Shouldn't.

That word scrapes against
the sides of my brain,
slides along the edges
of my intellect,
never fully piercing through,
but there
in the distance,
like a dream,
nonetheless.

We shouldn't do this.
It shouldn't happen.
I shouldn't go.

But I smell your scent,
a mixture of hand soap
and your own natural
earthy musk.
I've never smelled you before,
not once.
It's a strange and unfamiliar odor,
enticing and exhilarating.
It clouds my reason.

I take your hand, like a child
drawn by the promise of a treat,
of some reward,
letting my passion dictate,
ignoring warnings
that have been drilled
deep into my head
since I was young.

I take your hand
as you lead me away
from my comfort,
as your lure me into your parlor,
and tempt me with promises
left unspoken,
but implied.

Shouldn't.

It is right there in my mind.
My learned response,
my common sense,
my reason,
hovering just beyond the veil
of this heady intoxication,
lost in a haze of smoky,
wistful apprehension
and as good as forgotten
for now.

# My Favorite Face

That's my favorite face.

When your eyes are closed
and your teeth are clenched
and your lips are curled
just so,
that's my favorite face
of yours.

When you are the most raw,
your most open,
your most true,
the most you.

When your eyes roll
back
and your hair
is untamed, askew,
and your body tenses,
rigid,
and shakes,
and shivers
and all the world
disappears except
for us.

This is you.
Your most authentic,
most unguarded self,
open,
and alive,
and just,
for one eternal moment,
forgetting your carefully crafted
role.

Your countenance,
normally so prettied,
so painterly pristine,
is forgotten,
your make-up unkempt,
your eyeliner smeared,
your lipstick well worn away
from lips smashing haphazardly against lips.
And all traces of your perfected

play-acting and
role-playing and
living up to an image,
an appearance so manicured.
so intensely realized,
and so typically attended to,
it is all gone now
in this one moment,
this shuddering moment,
this quivering instant,
this eternity
in a whisper.

This is you.
The secretest you.
The caged you,
set loose, accidentally
in a spasm,
in a wave,
a you so pure,
so real,
so beautiful,
and yet so constrained,
that very few will
ever be so fortunate
as to see her.

# Your Windmill

I sit as close
to you
on the edge of the bed
as you
will allow,
wishing I could
reach out and
dry tears,
wishing tired eyes,
red and weary,
would return my gaze
once more,
wishing your hand
would touch mine,
would graze my skin,
would feel my heat,
would feel me.
Wishing you
would hear me.

But you don't.

And as I speak,
as I assure,
as I implore,
I feel you
go.

Not physically.
No.
You're here.
Mere inches away.
I feel your breath.
I hear you stifle
desperate sounds.
I smell your scent,
familiar and clean,
as much you
as ever.

But you're gone.

I'm the enemy
to you
now.

You've decided.
And there's no way
to convince you
it's simply not true,
to assure you
my allegiances,
my intentions,
are just as they've
always been.

I am a giant
to you
now,
suddenly,
looming large
on the horizon,
foul of brood,
with arms
nigh
two leagues in length.

I have become
in an instant,
nothing more than
a villain,
fearsome and threatening,
a monster
to be battled,
a threat
you must
protect yourself from
at all costs,
and I know
that you will come at me
with armor on,
at full gallop
raising your spear
high,
and ready to slay.

I wish that you
could hear me.
I wish that you
could see me
for what I am,
rather than what
you fear.
I wish that you

could retrace
your steps,
follow the breadcrumbs
back.
I wish that you
could go back
to that time,
mere minutes ago,
that time
before
I was
a giant.

# Dark Today

The sky is dark here today;
we're waiting for a rainstorm.

And I'm fighting a cold.
Actually, I haven't been sleeping well
        at all.

I got tickets to that premiere.

And my nephew can say his last name now.

These are just things
that I used to tell
you.

# The Spell

It's heartbreakingly sad,
that moment.

That one moment
you can pinpoint
as the exact moment
the spell
was broken.

The instant
when everything changed,
and the magic veil
that diffused
the harsh colors of your world,
was lifted away.

How intense
everything feels
without
the enchantment.

# Flesh and Bone

I'm here.

Right now.

Flesh and bone.
Flaws and scar tissue.
A muddle of qualities,
nuance,
and stark imperfection.

I'm standing right in front of you,
just like you were desperate for me to be.
And now your eyes look anywhere
        but mine.
Your lips, once hungry for my mouth,
        drip words of trivial origin.
Your hands, once desperate for my skin,
        busy themselves with idle action.

From thousands of miles away,
you longed for me

From inches,
you are dispassionate,
        removed.

I traveled so far to reach you,
invested so much
in the journey,
navigated so many obstacles,
waited patiently
to see your face,
and now the gulf between us
is wider
than any physical distance
could ever be.

# Muse

You are my muse
even in the death
of us,
an inspiration
even in your
absence.

# Junkie

When you ask
what I am thinking,
what is
on my mind,
at this
very
moment,
I wonder if it's
because
you sense
the confusion
in me.

How long
have we known
each other
now?
Three hours?
Not even three?
We're just
getting accustomed
to one another,
learning each other,
mere strangers.

And yet,
my very first thought
is of my utter,
unwarranted,
and palpable
desperation

for you.

You
are in front of me,
wrapped
in a black outfit
that looks
like skin.
And you
are standing
behind a table,
hip cocked,
bright lips

pursed,
stark against
pale skin,
and suddenly
this table
between us
is a barricade,
an obstacle,
a wall.
It leaves me feeling even
more
desperate
to get to you.
Ever
more
desperate
to have my
hands
on you.
To feel you
against me.
To take your face
between my palms
like a treasure,
to breathe in
the scent of you
and kiss you deeply,
as I shake
like a junkie,
missing a fix
I never realized
I craved.

I wonder
momentarily
if this
was the reaction
you expected,
you anticipated,
you longed for.
I wonder
momentarily
if you feel the same
desperation,
doubting
the chemistry
between us
only for the briefest

of moments,
before I remember
the shaking in my hands,
the perspiration on my face,
the twisting in my gut,
the ache in my bones,
this need,
this unstoppable
ravenous
hunger
for you.
And like the
unexpected fiend
that I am,
I push the table aside
violently,
moving recklessly
toward my prize,
and I know then –
seeing your eyes
come alive
watching your body
drift
subtly forward
to meet me –
I know
with all certainly
that you're
ready
to be consumed,
to be devoured,
to be taken in by me,
and to take me in,
just for now,
just for tonight,
not overthinking,
simply
letting the chemistry
work,
letting instincts
dictate
action,
and allowing
each of us
in this moment
to be
one another's
perfect
drug.

# Yes

Yes.

So much power
in just three letters.

Yes is vision.
Yes is power.
Yes is passion.
Yes is consent.

Yes...

And yet, it's so easy
to seek to add on to it.

Absolutely, yes.
Positively, yes.
A thousand times...yes.

But right now,
a simple
yes,
is all we need.

To add any more
is a disservice
to a beautiful
and precise
perfection.

Do you want to be in my space?
Yes.

Do I want your lips pressed to mine?
Yes.

Do you want to follow where I'll lead?
Yes.

Your hand on mine?
Your skin against my skin?
Our garments removed
and swept away?

Yes. Yes. Yes.

Do you want my full attention? Yes.
Do I want your tongue? Yes.
Do you want to hold each other closer,
ever closer,
until there is nowhere to go
but down?
Hands pulling tight against
exposed skin,
fumbling for undergarments,
wrestling covers away from
well made beds?

Yes.

Lips pressing feverishly,
teeth biting softly,
hands winding
through strands of tousled hair,
gripping limbs
and backs
for leverage,
for support,
as we inhabit
one another,
as we crawl inside
each other,
as we thrust
and sweat
and sigh...

Yes. Yes.

Yes.

Yes brings us here.
And it allows us to forget
to be afraid
to be fragile
to be self conscious.
It allows us to remember
to be present
to be awake
and alive
and aware
of every sensation,
every nerve ending,
every gasp,

every flutter,
every moan.

Yes.

It is the key to a hidden lock,
the answer to a silent question.

And yes
is the only word
you and I need.

For now.

# Dust

We are
fragile things,
mere dust,
cobbled from stars,
rocketing through space
at staggering speeds,
infinitesimal
compared
to the immensity
of the universe,
the complexity
of design.

We are but dust.
Living in a world
crowded with danger,
awash in peril,
a dominion,
it sometimes seems,
for malevolent things.

And every rational thought says,
"Be afraid."
Every inclination
should be
to cower,
to dread,
to be selfish,
to shrink back
from this life.

Yet we are brave,
this dust.

We stand
boldly
and we face the world.
We seek out the light
where there is darkness,
clarity
where there is chaos,
and love
where there is fear.

And there is no braver act
than love.

Than allowing our souls,
our spirits
to be exposed,
to be raw,
vulnerable,
when there is already
so much
at stake.

To say yes
to risk,
to recognize
ourselves
in another,
and to give
purely,
selflessly,
to form bonds
and families
when others
would have us believe
that is mere folly,
that there is too much at stake,
that we must wait
until all conditions
are secure,
until the safety net is strung up
below us,
ready to break our fall.

But those conditions will not exist.

We know that.
And yet we brave to love.

This dust.

We don't wait
to fall.
We jump
together,
holding hands,
growing old,

walking
side by side
through this world.

In doing so,
we risk,
yes,
but we also embrace
the thing that makes us
human,
unique and connected,
all at once,
two souls on one journey,
and we are rewarded so.

From beginning
until the end,
from dust to dust,
we brave
this world
together.

# If Darkness Descends

If my heart were to collapse
and burn...
If my breath were to cease,
and my eyes to fall shut...
If I were to begin to feel my light escape...
I wouldn't turn to you.

But I would weep for the idea.

If my hands were to quiver
beyond my control,
and my balance were to fail me...
If my mouth were to run dry,
and my knees to buckle beneath my weight...
I wouldn't let you know.

I would remain silent.

I would hold on to a memory of you.
I would embrace it...this fiction of you.
I would hold it against my cheek like silk
and whisper "thank you."

And even if my eyes were to roll back gently,
and my vision were to fade away,
and my skin were to chill,
I would cling to this idea of you in my mind
like a child
unable to let go

of a dream.

# The Bouquet

I passed through the
security checkpoint
at the tiny airport
in a daze.

I was relieved
to be headed home,
nursing the failure
of the weekend,
the disappointment
of promises left
unfulfilled.

"Is this yours?"
the security woman asked,
pointing to
a tiny
bouquet
of pink flowers
sitting neatly in the middle
of a security tub.

I shook my head.
It wasn't mine.

She asked the others around me
but no one stepped forward.
No one claimed it
as their own.

Just another beautiful thing
someone's leaving behind.

# Whim

I fear seeing you again
almost as much as
I long for it.

I know it will happen,
and I am disquieted
by the idea
that you may continue
to hold
sway
over me,
that you will continue
to grip me
at my core,
and that you will
lead me
to your bed
on a whim
and that I
will follow.

# Chemistry

I am perplexed,
bewildered,
by the arcane science
of you and me.

No diagram
can decipher the intricacies
of our equation.
No compound, no elixir,
can replicate
the subtleties of us.

I am befuddled
by the rapidly changing rules,
the shifting reality of this math;
remainders that do not equal
into the formula.

Molecules move between,
heat carries life,
and energy binds us
in ways we cannot decipher,
and cannot possibly
hope to escape.

# A Clean Execution

Final meal,
final thoughts,
final words,
and then it's time.

Time to remove you
from my world,
to expunge
your very existence.

Time to wipe away
your fingerprints.
Even memories of you
will quickly fade.

I will administer
the drugs myself,
and hold your hand
as you drift away.

I will wait until
you're gone,
and then clean up
what remains of you.

I'm a tidy
executioner.
I will leave
no trace.

I will scrub
the evidence of you away
from every aspect
of my life.

# Serpentine

Slipping...
        like a thief
        through a doorway
        in my mind.

Sliding...
        beneath the surface
        of my reflective pool.

Symbols, etched like a warning
run the length of her spine,
Snaking...
        back and forth beneath me.

Radiant heat illuminates the darkness of my bed,
a glistening damp hides the subtlety of our skin,
Desperation arrives.  Need.

My fingers pull tight the strands of tousled hair,
My mouth finds comfort in the soft curve of her neck,
Her sighs mix with my blood, throbbing behind my ears.

Like an admonition, the rune's twist...
my nails claw at the length of her taut back, begging them away.
But as if an incantation, my eyes return to them again and more...
        more.

Slithering...
        she winds her way around my chest
        until I cannot inhale.  Until the very breath of my reason
        is surcease.

I bite deep into the fruit of life, and ignore the serpent
as it moves and coils in front of my eyes...
        mocking me.

But it's too late.
Desperation and heat combine to overwhelm.
I need the knowledge...
bring the pain.

# Your Glory

Take my hand
and step over here,
right here
in front of me,
and let the fabric fall away.

Let my gaze
wash over you,
bathe you.

Don't turn away,
don't shrink back and be
small,
small like you're feeling
inside.

Breathe, instead.
Breathe
and be glorious
in your skin.

Is this,
perhaps,
can this be
the first time
a man
has taken in
your
nakedness
so completely,
so confidently,
inhaled you
like a
heady
fragrance,
drunk deeply
of you,
and savored you
like wine?
Is this
the first time
you've ever been
adored?

Don't be afraid.

It's all
potential
now,
unlimited possibility
for touch
and sensation,
unyielding capacity
to feeling
human.

Allow it
to be
as it is
herein this moment,
when all time
stands still
and judgments
are suspended.

Allow it
to be
as it is
without
scrutiny,
absent
self-recrimination,
freeof all
doubt.

There will be
plenty
of time
for doubt,
years
for judgment,
a lifetime
to spend
cultivating
an illusion
of disaffected
narcissism.

For now,
allow it.

Allow
your glory.
Embrace

your beauty.
And shine
like you're
alive.

# Ready

Be still
and wait there.

Wait for me.

Right there.
Just like that.

Still.
And perfect.

Don't move.
Just be there in the darkness.
And listen.
And wonder.
And wait...

I want you ready.

I want you
chomping at the bit,
wired,
and at your
wit's end.

I want you
      tensed
      and taut.
      Skin alive.
      Mind racing.
Impatient.
Anxious.
Tortured.

And ready.

      Teeth clenched
      in anticipation.

I want you
      second guessing
      every movement
      in the room,
      every breath
      of air

that glances
your cheek,
every sound.

Ready.

I want you
holding still,
bracing yourself,
senses alive.
Aching.

I want you
feeling phantom kisses
on every inch
of your
exposed skin.

I want you
ready to cry out,
short of breath,
heart racing,
nerves on fire,
unable to contain
your anticipation,
perspiration,
excitement,
a sense of breathless wonder,
a longing,
a need,
ready to burst forth
from within,
ready to spill out
of you
like a scream.

I want you.

Are you ready?

Let's begin.

# Vanished

If I disappeared,
would you go looking for me?

Would my absence
affect you
enough
to put your burdens down,
to lay your obligations aside
and seek me?

If I vanished,
would you worry?
Would you fret
and wring your hands?

About me?
And my safety?
And my ability to be lost
in this world
all on my own?

Or more,
about whether
I'd want
to be found
by you
at all?

# I Am Fire

I am fire.

All-consuming.
Voracious.
Unquenchable.

I am heat.

Living flame.

A furnace,
full of white
intensity,
devouring
everything I touch,
reaching out
with smoldering tendrils
to pull
the unsuspecting
deep
into my fiery
maw.

I am hungry.

Always
hungry.

And I must feed.

# Indestructible

I wash myself clean
in the steam of a shower
too hot for reason.

I scrub hard to shed
a thick layer of dead skin,
exposing the lustrous new scales
hidden beneath.

I stare at dark, glistening eyes
in a half-fogged mirror
through a misty haze,
and smile at the thought of her.

Trying so hard to protect me
from herself.
I was like a baby, she said,
unrestrained in a moving car;
I'd given her too much.

But here I am,
defenses firmly intact,
watching my naked form in the mirror,
a tinge of a buzz still in my head,
indestructible.

She will expect calls that will not come.
She will wonder about where I may be.
She will come to me, smiling
and then accuse me of hiding.

And she never had any idea
of what
I was capable.

But I'm right here;
potent,
obstinate,
unstoppable.

Say hello.

# Time Capsule

There was a package
waiting for me
today.
Addressed to me,
it smelled like you.
Inside was
a memento,
hand made;
the words
"desperately waiting,"
signed
"with love."

You must've sent it
before everything
changed.

Now, it feels
like a mere
curiosity,
an antique,
faded
and irrelevant,
a time capsule
from a forgotten day
when life was good
and everything
made sense.

# Your Lips

The sounds of the restaurant
recede
and I focus on your lips,
beautifully formed
looking somewhat soft,
and dripping with words
that I take in
and relish.

I focus on your mouth.
My gaze hovers
between it and
your eyes,
intense
and earnest
and startling.

I ignore the pronounced
collarbone
peeking out
from under
a flimsy cotton
top.

I ignore the swell
of your breast,
the punctuation of
rosebud nipples
against light fabric.

I ignore the envy I feel
as your hair bobs,
delicately caressing
the skin
of your smooth cheeks.

I ignore the throbbing
in my jaw,
the desire behind it
to kiss
and bite
and savor.

I ignore the heartbeat
in my ears.

And I listen.
And I watch your lips.
And I take you in,
each and every
delicious
word.

# That Night We Talked

We talk
so hard.

And I wonder...
are we really so frightened
of tenderness?
Are we so afraid
of real feelings
that we dive so easily
into matters
of flesh?

It's an easy enough thing,
to consummate.
But what are
we consummating
at all?

Cheap.
You said you felt
cheap.
Wasn't that the word
you used?

Well, you're right.
We are
cheap.

So much so
that we'd rather
sacrifice our bodies
to avoid paying
with our hearts.

Talk
is cheap.

# Learning You

Do I love you?

I'm only just
learning you,
soaking
in the knowledge
of who you are,
bathing
in the feel
of you.
And I love what I see.
I love how my soul feels
in proximity
to yours.
I love the way my breath
catches
in my throat
at the sight of you,
at the sound
of your voice.
I love how the world
drops away
when you speak
to me.
And
most of all
I love who I am
in your presence,
who I desire to be
in your eyes.

Do I love you?

No.

Not just yet.

But I long to.

# Daydreams

When I begin to get melancholy
about you,
about the loss of you
from my life,
I must remind myself that
you
were never actually real,
and one
cannot mourn
daydreams.

# Home Again

I pulled the coat tight around me
as the rain danced on my face,
dropped from my nose,
my lips.

All I could think of
was you,
was home.

A chill ran through me
as I waded through dirty puddles
and felt the grime on my legs,
splashed gelid and wet.

And my thoughts of you,
waiting for me,
and home.

The heat came too slowly in my car.
My teeth chattered
behind numbed cheeks.
My hands were on the steering wheel,
braving a wintry chill
with no gloves for protection.

But my mind was on you,
the warmth of you
beside my fire.
Hot chocolate and old movies,
and the feel of you close to me,
helping me warm cold limbs.

Your face is sanctuary,
home and dry
and safe
again.

# Muddled

damn
your muddled thoughts

ambiguous inclinations
tentative assertions
of interest
and desire

so fragile are these
threads
of gossamer
that connect us
ready to snap

I feel you
withdrawing
slowly
into the darkness
disappearing
from view

but I am not that man
and you are not that woman
anymore

don't deny us the chance
to make
our own
disastrous
mistakes

# Cannibal

I want to strip you down,
all of you,
and see what makes up
the sum of you,
the sum of parts,
all of your parts.

I want to dissect you,
to search
deep
beneath your skin,
and examine every inch
of tissue,
every ounce of flesh,
outside and in,
assessing and treasuring,
each muscle,
each vital organ,
every weighty thought.

I want to taste you,
each bit,
savoring the flavor of you,
each part unique,
dancing on my tongue.

I want to eat you whole.

# Phantom

I dance with a shadow...
>> her hips close to mine,
>> her hand lightly on my shoulder,
>> her breath on my cheek.

I move in time with a phantom...
>> here for mere moments,
>> impossible to contain,
>> intangible to my embrace.

I feel her presence envelop me...
>> warm whispers in my ear,
>> fuel for my aspiration,
>> elevating my joy.

Then gone.

Like a soft touch of wind on a summer's day,
a rustling of the trees,
the subtle hint of honey on my tongue,
the vague promise of winter in the air.
>> Fleeting.

Sweet apparition...
>> arriving at times of her choosing,
>> leaving no trace when she vanishes
>> save for her scent on my skin.

Expectations beg disenchantment;
all implied covenants will go unfulfilled.
She walks along a hooded path,
evanescing in and out of long shadows.

I'm ready to follow...
>> but she will not show me the way.

# The Dress

You appear
from around the corner
in that dress
and my logic
freezes;
I feel dizzy,
dazed,
starved.
That dress,
my,
that dress;
so tightly hewn,
all curves and soft fabric and black,
and blacker still
against your smooth,
alabaster skin;
as if it's a tattoo,
only painted on,
flattering every bend
in you,
dutifully hiding away
all the secret parts
of you,
and still,
just low enough
to offer a window,
a hint,
a promise,
just short enough
to permit
the tops
of your tight
black stockings
to sneak out,
to peek out,
to tease.
I see you
in that dress
and I flush,
I falter,
I forget
that I am civilized,
a gentleman.
This image of you
tickles

my reptilian brain,
tugs
at the very
root
of my passion;
it makes me weak
for you,
for this world.
You
are an inspiration,
in this moment,
a moment for which
documentation
was created.
This image,
your image,
demands
to be saved
to the hard drive,
pressed into a book
of precious
photographs,
painted on canvas,
etched on the walls
of dimly lit caves,
to be recalled
and savored
forever,
again and again,
as the very reason
we live.

# Sense Memory

Eyes locked,
hips swaying to incidental music;
far too many clothes.

Alcohol-tinged kisses.
Dim light,
just enough.

My hands know her curves, her lines,
      with no adjustment.
I breathe her in;
and she smells the same as she ever did,
      her aroma fills me up,
      makes me dizzy.

Her hair hangs over one eye,
      and she spies on us
      like an observer, like a voyeur,
      intrigued,
      pleased.
Sweet intoxicated smiles.

My mouth on her mouth,
her hand on my back,
my hand between her thighs.
"You're wet," I say, surprised.
"Are you here?" she asks, with assurance. "Then *yes*."
      Her insistent whispers reverberate in my head,
      warming my blood.

Petite footsteps across wooden floors,
      tracing a path
      to her bedroom;
      a path well traveled.

She holds my hand, and pulls me along,
      and I follow, clumsy in her wake.

There is no "what if?"
There is no "wait."
There is only now, here, please…
      yes.

And we fall into a rhythm.
Suspended,
      out of time.

Not *short* on time, but *out* of time,
Like two unstoppable objects on a collision course,
      unavoidable,
      bound together,
      locked,
      knowing, touching, holding,
      abandoning ourselves
      to one another,
      and together as one
      in certainty,
      and reverence.

I kneel at her altar,
And she mine,
      baptized in each other's sweat,
      swaddled in each other's skin.

"Never stop," she sighs, "just…never stop."
And I don't mind if I don't,
I don't mind
      if I stay
      right
      here.

# Skin

Smooth.
Your skin,
It's so smooth, and...

I'm sorry.

I know how you must hate me.
I know.

But...
I feel
the heat
between us
right now.

I watch your legs.
Your lips.
Your hair, so subtly framing.
I taste you in the air...

I'm sorry.

I'll move away.
But...you don't really want me to, do you?

No.
You look at me with eyes I know.
I touch you.
I feel your skin, warm under my fingertips.
I smell your hair, your neck.
My lips tingle as they brush your cheek.

And we kiss.

Pulling in close, and again.
Moving away, but back, and then again.
The heat of your mouth, the swell of your breast.
And your hands are in my hair, pulling me
closer than is possible.
Sighing.
Back. Forth.
I'm touching the skin of your thigh,
and I feel you shiver.
Your hands are on my back.
And suddenly, we're down.

On the floor, and again.
Lips cradling lips, and again.
Hot, lucid skin.
We put each other in this position, and now,
now, it is not our choice.
And again.

Skin against skin against skin, and again.
Sweat. And heat.
Lust. And love.
Moving, interlocked,
Carnal, corporeal...feral.
And again.
And again.
And again.

Two become one, and again.
Wrong becomes right, and again.
I'm biting into your neck because I do not know.
You're clawing at my back because you cannot think.
Wrapped and warmed, and again.
And again.
And again.
Until there is no consciousness, but collective.
No thought, only feeling,
and again.

I lose myself in you as ever before
and ever again,
and again.
My warmth into you and you around me, and again.
Skin against skin.
I wrap you in my arms,
collapsing in remission!
We too, and...again!
No. Yes.
Can't think.
Too much.
Not enough.
God!
Cannot breath, cannot move, cannot talk.
God, oh God.
And time stands still in you, and in I...

forever.

And then...
I can feel you again.

Your skin.

I smell our combined smells.
I feel your chest heaving under mine.

I can taste your skin.

Your smooth, beautiful, resplendent skin.
Your mask, your shield, your sense.
As if it was yesterday,
as it is now,
and as it might never be
          again.

# When

When
is enough?

Of you and I?
Inhaling the same air?
Sharing the same space?

I tiptoe across the floor,
taking tenuous steps,
afraid to wake the thing
slumbering
within us
that will say
too much.

Fragile touches of your face,
afraid to look
too deeply within
your eyes;
afraid that I might glimpse
something other
than affection.

If you've had enough
say when.

Of me
of us
of this…
say when.

If you've decided you're ready
to run
to fly
to escape the all too real…
then just
say
when.

I'm waiting…
unsure of everything.

And it's killing me.

Don't say it.
Please.

Don't ever
　　　say it.

# Precious Cargo

We moved too fast
carrying precious cargo,
not nearly cautious enough
about securing our payload.

We were headstrong, impervious,
driving recklessly into the storm,
cavalier about consequence,
and confident in our abilities.

But our fragile load
wasn't nearly as strong as we hoped;
it didn't survive the storm
unscathed.

For, in our recklessness, our hurry,
we failed to understand
the gravity
of the truth:
that some things,
once broken,
can never be mended.

# Kidnapped

Driving to a familiar place
I've never been.
Feeling your hand resting
on my thigh.
I glance over at you,
and you smile.

You're so pleasant
for a hostage.

The waves break close to shore.
The overcast sky is oddly comforting.
I have the need to feel the water,
the soft sand between my toes.
I imagine walking out into the void,
        disappearing.
I watch the tiny footprints of birds
tracked onto the beach.

I'm so glad you are here with me.
I needed you here.
Needed you to tell me things that I already knew,
to laugh at me, and to assuage my fear.

You tell me I'm strong.
That I can be weak with you,
and curl into your arms,
but that at the same time,
you'll be curling into mine,
protected by my strength.

To never forget who I am.

It all feels so extrinsic to me today.
It all feels so far away...
        except for you,
        right here
        in this place we never knew before.

# Language

We danced around it,
afraid of what it might be.

We attempted to fool ourselves.

As if, by refusing to label it,
it didn't truly exist,
didn't become real.

Because once real,
it was subject to the decay,
the entropy,
that we both understood so well.

So we avoided it,
even discussing it.

And yet it was real,
no matter what we called it,
it was exactly what it was destined to be.

Still delicate, friable,
still human,
and still bound to the laws of
our little universe...
no matter how much we attempted
to hold it outside our sphere
of understanding,
and elevate it.

We were still its architects.
We who are flawed and
uneducated.

No matter what language we used
to describe it,
it was still going to become exactly
what we were capable of building...

A beautiful sanctuary
built on a faulty foundation,
and destined to be
temporary.

# If I Were

If I were a painter...
> I would spread my paints
> across an empty canvas,
> swirling dazzling hues into a coalescence
> of thought and desire.

If I were a sculptor...
> I would grasp wet earth
> between rough and agile fingers,
> creasing and folding God's foundation
> into a beautiful visage of form and function.

And if I were a musician...
> I would hold my instrument gently.
> I would tune my voice into readiness.
> I would let notes build into chords and merge
> into a flowing stream of grace,
> a song of lyric illusion; a celebration
> of my life, my love, my inspiration.

But I am only a poet...
> I have only my words to lay before you,
> only a piece of paper as my canvas,
> only imagination as my clay,
> and only my mind as my instrument.
> I rely merely on cadence and verse
> to convey the melody of my thoughts;
> the syncopation of my semantics
> to persuade you that my music is true.

I am simply a writer...
I offer these parts of me to you...
I lay them before you with no accompanying arrangement,
with no pedestal or frame with which to display them.

I offer you only my words,
but they are yours.
Take them from me...
> if you will.

# Temporary

I sigh.

I know that look,
the one in your eyes
         right now.

It means you're restless.
That you've grown
dissatisfied.
That you are ready for something
         more
than what we have
at this very moment,
the next step,
a hard turn onto a path
that I never had interest
in traveling.

I know that look.
It's the prelude
to the shrugs and the frowns
and the inevitable
rambling conversations
which begin with deep,
exasperated breaths
and end with bruised feelings,
stained faces,
and goodbyes.

I know that look.
I've seen it before.
It means the end of all of this.

We both knew
that this was only ever going to be
         temporary.
That I would never be the one
to kiss you deeply
in front of an audience of your choosing,
never be the one
standing next to you
in hanging portraits
on freshly painted walls,
never be the one
to hold your hand

patiently
while the end credits rolled.

We both knew
that we were always
          destined
to be mere passengers on this
subway car,
sharing stories
and smiles
and laughter,
a brief connection
between stops.

But nevertheless,
I sigh.

Because the ride was far shorter
than I would've liked.

Because it seems to me
that there are still more stories
we need to tell,
more laughter
we need to share.

Because I continue to enjoy you,
to revel in the experience
of you.

And I wasn't ready
for it to end
just yet.

# Version

The touch of your skin
is like velvet.
The warmth of your breath
on my neck
makes me numb.
This dream of you
envelops me,
and a phantom smell of you
fills my head
like a familiar,
comfortable,
intoxicating
lie.

I try to reach out
and pull you close to me,
but the memory of you
disappears
like smoke.

You're only you
in my memories now,
the version of you
that I believed in,
the version of you
that I trusted,
the version of you
that I allowed myself
to love.

That version of you
didn't ever truly exist.

I made her.

I only gave her everything
because I knew
she wouldn't accept.

# Once

Do you remember when you loved me once?

Do you remember those times
when you were thrilled
to hear my voice
and I hung on your every word?
When we made each other laugh
and challenged each other's ideas?
When it was enough to just be
        together,
listening to each other breathe?
When we counted the moments before we could speak again
with eager
anticipation?

Do you remember?
When you loved me once?

Cast your memory back
a day or two.

# Truth

I love you, baby.

Simple words.
Am I sincere?
Are you?

As the words drip from your lips
like delicate drops from a perfect folded leaf...
do you believe them?

Hot breath steams gelid night air;
it obscures our vision like a haze.
The smoke from a slowly burning cigarette
curls around our heads like halos.
The darkness of the porch wraps us
in an embrace, closing in tight.
Stars that are simply too bright
provide our only illumination.

I love you, baby.
With my hands tied up in your hair,
the words are real.
There is no dishonesty on my warm tongue
as it traces the curve of your throat.
There is no confusion in lust.

My heart believes every word you whisper,
and my eyes meet yours in a gaze
that is the very definition of naked
            honesty.

Exposed skin tingles with electricity,
caressed by the cold of the night.
Fingers run a course over soft flesh;
nails meet bone, muscles become rigid
under sinewy hands.

I love you, baby.
You love me too.
This is truth.
We need not look for more.

# Shades

From the glow
of the incandescents,
spilling warm light
across the furniture,
the fabric,
projecting
hazy caramel shadows
on cream-colored walls –
and you there,
reclining
on the loveseat,
blanket covering
your tiny feet,
coffee mug gripped
with two hands
near your face,
hair up,
your face fresh
and clean,
beautiful
in your natural state.

To the brilliant radiance
of the midday sun spilling
through plantation shutters,
casting slowly shifting patterns
on rough wooden floors,
warming them
with welcoming light –
and your voice carries
from the kitchen,
echoing through the room,
softly humming a tune
that meant something
to us
then.

To the departing light
of dusk,
leaving a mere hint
of the day behind,
a cotton candy caress
across the features
of the room –
you're at the table,

headphones on,
silently writing,
your foot tapping
a steady rhythm
on the sturdy wrought iron
of the
barstool.

And to the candlelight
casting
long shadows
on hungry faces,
rich amber patterns
dancing,
obliquely lit,
tiny flames reflected
in dark anxious eyes
as familiar music plays
on the speakers
in the background,
deep and insistent.
You are
looking at me
earnestly,
stripped down
to your barest
desire.

This room shifts
hourly,
bathed in light
and life,
nuance
and identity,
a slowly altering
palette
of color.
And the memory
of you
is imbued
in each
and every
shade.

# Why Do You Love Me?

"Why do you love me?" she asked.

"Is it for my style,
the way I dress,
even when, inside,
I feel like a child
in her mother's clothes?

Is for my personality,
the jokes I make,
the stories I tell,
the confidence I project,
even when I feel like an imposter?

Is it for the way I work
to keep my muscles taut,
my body firm,
my skin smooth,
my hair coiffed,
even when I feel so ugly,
so frail,
so fragile?

Is it for the way I laugh
even when I'm close to tears?
For the way I'm cool
even when I'm struggling?
For the way I'm calm
even when I'm close to screaming?

Is it for my kindness
even when I feel so angry
and lost?

Or for the smile I wear
even when
I'm breaking
inside?"

"No," I said,
pulling her close,
touching her lips
to mine.

"I love you

because I see you.

I see you
just as you are,
strong and fragile
all at once,
a beautiful, amazing
juxtaposition,
bold,
yet breakable.

I love you
not in spite of,
but because."